Hello! ITSMEEE Again...

By
Patricia A. Fisher

Published by
ITSMEEE™ Industries
Aurora, Colorado
USA

Patricia A Fisher

Copyright © 2002 by Patricia A. Fisher
Published by ITSMEEE™ Industries

All rights reserved, including the right to reproduce this book or portions
thereof in any form. No part of this book covered by the copyrights
hereon may be reproduced or copied in any form or by any means –
graphic, electronic, or mechanical, including but not limited to,
photocopying, recording, taping, scanning, or information storage and
retrieval systems – without the express written permission of the author,
Patricia A. Fisher.

Front cover art and all interior art by Patricia A. Fisher
Cover design and book layout by NZ Graphics, Lakewood, CO

Printed in the United States of America

First Edition

Library Of Congress Control Number: 2002112925
Old ISBN: 0-9677231-1-6
New ISBN: 978-0-9677231-1-2

Other Titles by Patricia A. Fisher

With Love ITSMEEE™
Copyright © 1997 by Patricia A. Fisher

With Love ITSMEEE™ II
Copyright © 1998 by Patricia A. Fisher

Introducing Number III, ITSMEEE™
Copyright © 1999 by Patricia A. Fisher

ITSMEEE™ On My Journey Home
Copyright © 1999 by Patricia A. Fisher
ITSMEEE™ Industries

Hello, ITSMEEE™ Again
Copyright © 2002 by Patricia A. Fisher
ITSMEEE™ Industries

Patricia A Fisher

Other Titles (Continued)
By Patricia A. Fisher

ITSMEEE™ Beneath the Grey
An Autobiography
Copyright © 2003 by Patricia A. Fisher
ITSMEEE™ Industries

From This Day Forward
Copyright © 2003 by Patricia A. Fisher
ITSMEEE™ Industries

I Want to LIVE!
Copyright © 2004 by Patricia A. Fisher
ITSMEEE™ Industries

Walk a Mile in Our Shoes
Copyright © 2005 by Patricia A. Fisher
ITSMEEE™ Industries

Hello ITSMEEE Again

Other Titles (Continued)
By Patricia A. Fisher

The Favor I Owe the World
Copyright © 2005 by Patricia A.
Fisher
ITSMEEE™ Industries

Home Is Where We Park It!
Copyright © 2008 by Pat Fisher
Funhous Publishing

The Absence of Awful
Copyright © 2012 by Patricia A.
Fisher
ITSMEEE™ Industries

Patricia A Fisher

Table of Contents:

DEAR READER, ... x
IN LOVING MEMORY OF OUR MOM, ... 2
MY MAMA AND ME 7
MY FIGHT FOR FREEDOM 14
THIS IS MY PLEA 17
FOR MY GOOD DOCTOR 19
TRIBUTE TO DEE 25
MY DEAREST DEE 29
TILL WE MEET AGAIN 33
A CRUMPLED SHEET OF PAPER 36
ALL BUT MY SOUL 41
THE CLOSENESS I SEEK MAY NEVER BE… 47
CHRISTMAS 53
ON THE ROAD 59
THE HEALING OF NATURE 63
HOME SICK PUP 70
LITTLE BIRDIE 71
NATURE'S MUSIC 72
A GOLDEN MOMENT 76

Hello ITSMEEE Again

Table of Contents Con't:

AGGRAVATION! 78
RACHEL AT 17 82
THE "C" WORD 85
YOU CAN'T RUN FOREVER 89
ONLY YESTERDAY 95
GOODBYE, MOM… 101
EARTH: A PLACE BETWEEN.... 103

Patricia A Fisher

When someone is "in the pits",

We dare not "jump in" after him (in the name of rescue or love, etc.)

He must, first, "reach up", and hopefully, someone will be there to pull him the rest of the way out.

If the one person "jumps in" to save the other, all we would end up with is: two people "in the pits", instead of one!

– P. A. Fisher

Support = Helping someone help himself.
– Dee Stanley

Hello ITSMEEE Again

Patricia A Fisher

Dear Reader Most Kind,

Journaling in Rhyme has been my own way to put personal thoughts on paper since I was age 15.

Putting all of this into book form is my way of sharing what it is like to be a human being with schizophrenia.

Having this affliction is different from a lot of other diseases.

When a person has headaches, allergies, or even old age, it is socially acceptable for them to talk to other people about it.

x

Hello ITSMEEE Again

When a person has a mental disorder, stigma makes them stay silent. This makes mental illness a very lonely disease.

I envy people who go on television to speak about a problem they have. They may not realize that this sharing, they are doing, is a gift. It keeps them connected to people, which is a huge step toward the cure, or management, of their particular difficulty.

When a person has a mental disorder, like mine, they have fewer places to connect with others. Even friends, and family, shy away from the subject.

I can't just say to people, "Oh, no! My schizophrenia hurts today."

Patricia A Fisher

When I speak about it, people go silent.

It is as if there is a huge purple elephant in the room, and no one acknowledges its presence! I once lost an eighteen-year-old friendship, because of sharing a thought with my friend.

I'm not saying my schizophrenia is worse than any other illness. How can you measure? I am just telling you it is a lonely place to be.

Hence, my books are my way of connecting with myself, my family, and the rest of the world.

While you read, you may notice that I am a lot like you. You may notice that I, too, am just another human being. (As are others with illnesses like mine.)

Hello ITSMEEE Again

We no longer want to sit among other people and stay silent about our particular challenges or triumphs.

My books have been my way of sharing with all people – not only a select few. I feel they have meaning for everyone.

Maybe you will feel less alone from reading them. Maybe you will get a chuckle a time or two...Set aside an hour and enjoy reading them slowly.

*Be with me, as I say goodbye to my **amazing** Mom.*

*And be with me while I say goodbye to Dee Stanley. Dee was my wonderful and **precious** counselor for many years.*

Patricia A Fisher

Again,
I thank you
for being a part
of my journey

Patricia A.
Fisher

Hello ITSMEEE Again

There

Are

No

Little

People...

Patricia A Fisher

IN LOVING MEMORY OF OUR MOM,

Constance Marie Holley
June 27, 1924 – November 18, 2001

Hello ITSMEEE Again

My mother and I felt a huge love for each other, but I never could get her to admit I was the favorite of her five daughters!

Mom and I fought like cats and dogs, and we laughed just as hard.

She was a warrior in her battle to obtain more from life. (More than just the pain handed to her at birth.)

There are many things she gave me. One is an indispensable love of little things. The second is my own warrior – like strength to survive.

Patricia A Fisher

Within the piece, "My Mama and Me," I speak of our pool. I want to share that our pool was built by Mom and Dad alone. They used cement and flagstone (a pick and a shovel, most likely).

They created a fairly large, kidney-Shaped pool (four feet deep with three steps at one end).

My sisters and I spent many joyful days and evenings in that pool. I believe we all four learned to swim in it.

Hello ITSMEEE Again

Before mom's death, I forgave her and dad for any atrocities they may have shed on me.

*Well, mom and dad, this forgiveness may have helped you **and** me.*

Your mistakes, fears, confusion, anger, and even love, only speak of all humanity, and how we fall short of being perfect. I hope you both have passed on to a place of love and kindness, and that you at last possess peace of mind.

You did your best. I'm proud of you both.

With love,
ITSMEEE
Number 3

Patricia A Fisher

Our Dad Lester W. Holley

Hello ITSMEEE Again

MY MAMA AND ME
(Reprinted from *ITSMEEE On My Journey Home*)

Just what can I do for you? My
Mama said to me.

I wish that I could help you more.
That's how I want to be.

You are very dear and good.
My love, I make this vow,

I would give my life for you,
If you would ask me now.

I would sell my jewels,
I would sell my gold.

What else can I do for you?
My love for you untold.

Patricia A Fisher

The day that I gave birth to you,
I just could never say

The wonder and the miracle
God gave me on that day.

My answer, "Mom, just care for me,
Your love is all I need."

Listen when I talk to you,
This is what I plead

Hold me when I cry, sweet Mama.
Do what you do best.

Share what you have learned of old,
I don't need all the rest.

Hello ITSMEEE Again

Your gold, and all your jewels,
Though I tease you so,

I just want you to be there,
But also you must know,

That you will live within my heart,
If you have to go.

If you have to leave me, Mom,
I just want you to know,

You taught me joy of little things,
Of music and of fun,

Of being good to elders,
And good to everyone,

Patricia A Fisher

Of just to look upon a tree,
Or a mountain or a stream,

Or animals and flowers,
Remember real cream?

You and dad saw to it
That we all had a pool,

Hence, my love of water,
Fresh and wet and cool.

So be at rest my darling,
For you have given me,

So much I can't repay you.
So much love have we.

Hello ITSMEEE Again

If you go before me,
I want that you should know,

I'll remember everything –
And ice cream made of snow.

Don't hang on, my darling,
If the pain is getting bad,

I've had the best of mothers
Anyone has ever had….

Patricia A Fisher

I have found my mom and dad. In other words they were lost to me until I forgave them. I realized that I forgave them for being human.

Hello ITSMEEE Again

I *used to think that God caused the bad stuff, as well as the good.*

Now that I know, in my heart, He only does good stuff, I can talk with Him anytime I want.

God doesn't do mean things – even to teach me a lesson.

Patricia A Fisher

MY FIGHT FOR FREEDOM

In front of me people were
talking loud.
Behind me it was the same.

The power that was guiding me
I knew was not a game.

I took a moment to calm the fear
That was welling up inside.

No way could I still the trembling.
Their power could not be denied.

Hello ITSMEEE Again

I stayed in control of the demons
That came from inside my brain.

But this power all around me
Made me see I had nothing to gain

By fighting back, or acting out,
Or telling them, "Now be gone!"

They wouldn't hear
Year after year.

Their force seems to go
On and on….

Patricia A Fisher

It's been a long, long time,
That I have prayed for peace,

That I have tried
Most everything

To get the pain to cease.
Tomorrow is another day.

I hope, and pray, to see,
That I can do

Just what it takes,
To help myself pull free...

Hello ITSMEEE Again

THIS IS MY PLEA

Let us be an instrument
Of peace, and love, and truth.

And let us share the laughter
That sustained us in our youth.

Our world needs lots of nurturing
To heal some ugly scars.

Sometimes to keep from feeling bad
Let's gaze upon the stars.

Because we need each other,
To help ourselves survive,

Let's hold onto each other
Love will help us thrive ...

This is my plea.
  Patricia A. Fisher

Patricia A Fisher

I've talked
To so many people
Privately
That everybody
Knows
My business...

Hello ITSMEEE Again

FOR MY GOOD DOCTOR

I cried again today,
Because you're going away.

You'll still be in my heart,
When we are far apart.

God sends his little angels
To warm us in the cold.

To guide us when we're weary.
To help our dreams unfold.

Patricia A Fisher

I hope it is ok
That I tell you today
"God bless you
As you go.
You may already know
That you'll be missed,
 And I insist

That you take care,
And you beware
Of any danger
In the world
That you may come upon.

Call me, I will be there
Until it is all gone.

Hello ITSMEEE Again

I wish for you sweet dreams,
And love from family.
Be close, and warm.
Wait out the storm.
Safe and sound you'll be.

For you are such an angel –
One of the very best.
You live a life of service,
And you deserve a rest.

Patricia A Fisher

Say "hey" to all your folks up
there (up North Dakota way).
Give them my love,
And God's above,
Be happy, this I pray.

See ya, little angel.
You took good care of me.

Thank you, little angel.
I'm grateful as can be

That I ever met you
How softly you did walk,
A precious little angel,
Made of "Nodak" stock!

Sincerely,

Patricia A. Fisher

Hello ITSMEEE Again

Patricia A Fisher

Delores Stanley
May 31, 1940 – December 13, 2000

Hello ITSMEEE Again

TRIBUTE TO DEE

I first met Dee around 1981. Once during my first little while at CLP (Community Living Program), she called the police and made me apologize for cussing at her. This helped me to keep from "acting out" whenever I felt very upset, even to this day.

During all of this, I knew that she cared about me, and had my best interests at heart.

In those first years I found that I not only respected Dee, but I also loved her more and more as time went on.

I left CLP for a while and came back about five years ago.

Patricia A Fisher

I chose Dee for my therapist, and we started the most powerful therapy I've had in the 31 years I have had this challenge.

During this time I wrote four books and published them. I came to peace with the little child inside me who use to cause me so much pain.

With Dee's help, I faced fears that came from the very roots of my childhood.

*She helped me, and my mom, separate into two unique individuals, and she also helped me mend my **very** broken heart.*

Dee bought the very first book I sold, and was quite supportive around my selling more.

Hello ITSMEEE Again

*Whenever I asked Dee how she was, she always, **always** had something good to say.*

At these times, she would smile her beautiful smile with her eyes just sparkling.

Sometimes I thought she knew the secrets of life, when I looked upon her face.

Dee did a lot of good while she was on this planet, and I will miss her dearly.

Her words are forever in my thoughts, and the love, through her eyes, will stay in my heart.

Wherever you are, Dee, I love you.

Pat

Patricia A Fisher

Hello ITSMEEE Again

MY DEAREST DEE

Take my hand,
And walk beside me,
If only in my mind.

Difficulties
Don't abide me.
This is what I find.

Many hours
Have we spent
All the many years.

All the months
We sat together
Erasing all my fears.

Patricia A Fisher

You were there
In support
Of whatere' I would feel.

You were there
Helping me
From unreal into real.

I held your hands so tightly
One day, I don't know why
My fear, or something, made me,
As I let out a cry.

I remember only,
Holding on to you.
The rest was
Only darkness,
As fear inside me grew.

Hello ITSMEEE Again

You may have had
A busy day,
Or something
On your mind.

But there you were,
Completely.
My dear, you are so kind.

We work together
Very well.
Amazing what we've done!

Even through
The pain and tears,
We also had some fun

Patricia A Fisher

So my salute
To you is this –
Now that you
Are ill,

Take what you need
From others,
Until you've had your fill.

For you have given
Much to us
In, oh, so many ways!

May you also
Get some back,
And have some
Brighter days.

                    I love you,

                         Pat

Hello ITSMEEE Again

TILL WE MEET AGAIN

My lovely Dee
I miss you,
A human
Oh, so kind.

You left us
Very quickly,
But here on Earth
You shined!

As a person
How you prospered!
And, oh, the love
You gave!

I always tried
To give some back –
To be
So very brave,

Patricia A Fisher

To let you know
I heard you,
When you would
Say a word.

I tried to
Carry out
My work.
Yes, sweet Dee,
I heard.

I won't forget
A bit of it,
Of how you helped me so.

I'll have you
In my thoughts, and heart,
Until the day I go.

Some day
We'll speak
Again,
Sweet Dee.

Hello ITSMEEE Again

I'll ask you,
"How are you?"
You'll sing to me
Sweet sonnets.
Yes, that is what you'll do.

For you'll be free
Of sadness,
And filled
With joyous song.

So 'till we meet
Again, sweet Dee,
I must say,
"So long."

Patricia A Fisher

A CRUMPLED SHEET OF PAPER

A crumpled
Sheet of paper

I hold
Here in my hand.

You may not think
Significant,

You may not
Understand.

It brings about
A strength in me –

A power
Don't you see?

Hello ITSMEEE Again

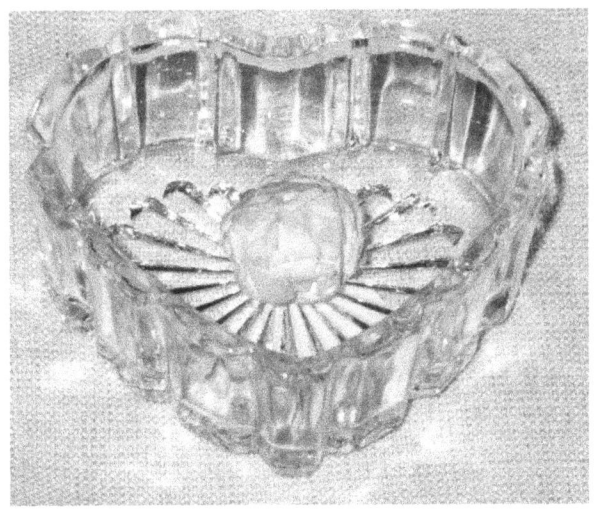

T'was handed
To me gently.

It helps
To set me free.

A crumpled
Piece of paper

Reminds me
That I am

Patricia A Fisher

A valid
Individual.

You may not
Understand.

No writing
On the face of it,

No writing
On the back.

Not a word
On either side.

But power
Didn't lack

Hello ITSMEEE Again

She gave it to me
With the words,

"Now go out
In the world.

You too
Can now be counted.

Your dreams
Are now unfurled.

This crumpled
Piece of paper

Will remind you
That you can

Be all
You want to be,
My love.

Just hold it
In your hand."

Patricia A Fisher

I met a soul while I was walking on my path.

It was mine . . .

Hello ITSMEEE Again

ALL BUT MY SOUL

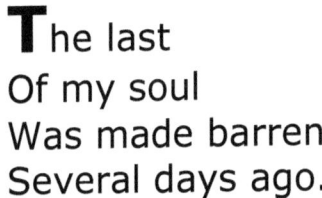

The last
Of my soul
Was made barren
Several days ago.

Nothing
For
Protection.

Stripped clean,
Had no
Friend or foe.

Patricia A Fisher

It stayed there
Inside my body.
Had no pride
Or self-contempt.
.

It stayed there
Inside my body.
To feel,
It seemed exempt.

Hello ITSMEEE Again

I kept my hand
On my chest
For fear
My soul would go.

Like every
Dream
I cherished,

And all
My tales
Of woe.

Patricia A Fisher

A million
Thoughts
And secrets,

I have
No more.
You see,

I've given
All
My treasures.

You ask
What's left
Of me?

Hello ITSMEEE Again

What's left
Just gives me life,
A thing
So hard to know.

It's plain
And simple.
I know it.

What's left
Is just
My soul.

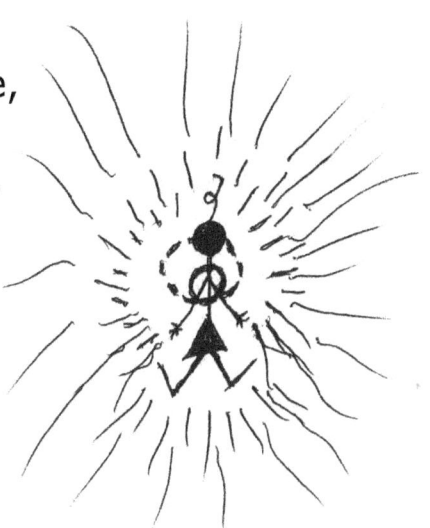

Patricia A Fisher

The reason we keep
Beating our heads against
The same wall, over and
Over again, is:

There is always
Hope.

Hello ITSMEEE Again

THE CLOSENESS I SEEK MAY NEVER BE...

I'm trying to hope
It seems you don't care
We've had broken hearts
No more dreams to share.

It hurts to the quick
The pain inside
Whenever we fight
My heart won't abide.

Our feelings are valid
We need to be heard
We withhold our love
Seldom saying a word.

Patricia A Fisher

We don't even speak
'Bout our Christmas gifts
We've traded around the tree.

We close ourselves off,
Each other we scoff.
This isn't the way
I want us to be.

A long time ago
When we were small,
Our mama hurt us bad.

Someone else
Got in the act.
I know it was
Our troubled dad.

I've gotten through
The walls I built
To save myself from them.

Hello ITSMEEE Again

They were human,
Limited,
Mistaken now and then.

So we have stayed
Away from each other
This caused us too much pain.

But if we don't
Get closer
Our love is all in vain.

People we've loved
Are passing away
One right after the other.

Our most recent loss
Is pain we must cross
We now have lost our mother.

Patricia A Fisher

I still want to try
To get closer than
"Hello" and then
"Goodbye."

Yet we must be true
To ourselves
Even if
Someone should die.

Hello ITSMEEE Again

More than nine times out of ten,
People are good people,
Just trying to keep their heads
above water...

Patricia A Fisher

My Dear Sweet
Master of All,
all my days are
prayers to you.

If there comes a
day when I do not
mention your name,
the very next day
I will speak of you
twice.

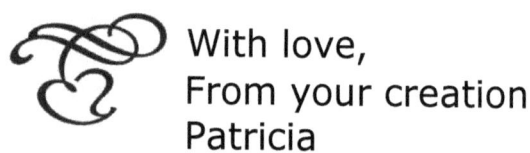 With love,
From your creation
Patricia

Hello ITSMEEE Again

CHRISTMAS

Christmas is
That time of year
When gifts
Are given away,

When stores
Are open
Late at night
And people are busy
All day.

To me it's a fine
Excuse to give
And share
What all we can.

From morning
'Till night
My mood is light.
I've love
For every man.

Monkey ↑ I tried for a Teddy Bear!

Patricia A Fisher

What'll I give to Mary?
Will this fit?
Or will that?

What will I send,
And then at the end
What about this hat?

My hubby says, "Bah Humbug!"
It's hard to drag him along
To every affair,
From here and to there,
To shows, and dances and song.

Why he doesn't feel it –
The joy I have inside,
The way I feel,
When sharing is real.
He wants to run and hide!

Hello ITSMEEE Again

The lights and music
Fill my heart
With praise upon my lips.

Thank you, God
For this old bod
And for the frost that nips.

For this abundance that I feel
When Christmas
Comes my way.

Patricia A Fisher

It feels so good,
I knew it would.
Thank you for this day.

Hello ITSMEEE Again

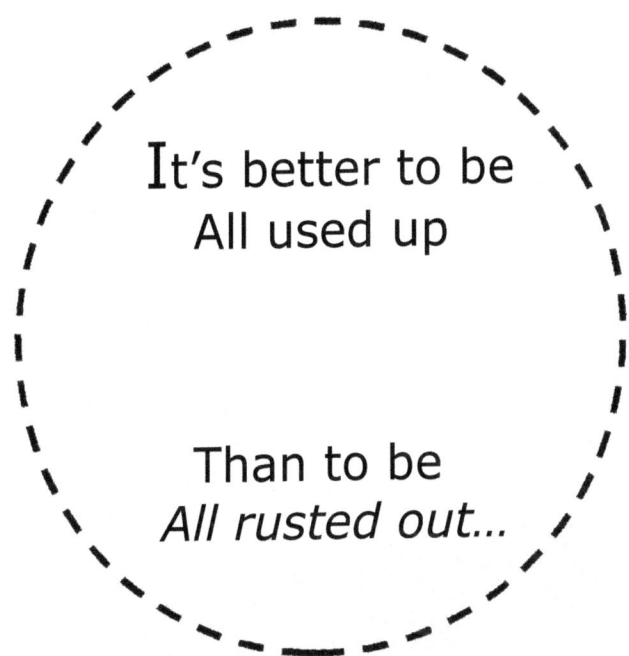

It's better to be
All used up

Than to be
All rusted out...

Patricia A Fisher

ON THE ROAD

Hello ITSMEEE Again

ON THE ROAD

"Dangerous crosswinds,"
It said on the sign.

If you keep on going,
You may just find

Your car or RV
Will toss and turn

You'll be so scared
And your tires will burn.

You may even die
As your vehicle rolls.

They'll put up a cross,
And they'll bless your souls.

If you make it through
The wind and the rain,

Patricia A Fisher

You might find yourself
In a mood to complain.

"Why was there only
A tiny sign

To warn us and tell us
What 'ere' we would find?

Build us a wall,
On the side of the street,

Or maybe some trees
Could be planted in peat,

Something to slow
The wind cross the road

So we can get home
To our humble abode."

The reason is clear
  Why these things are not done,

Hello ITSMEEE Again

Not enough money
To save everyone!

So they put up a sign
To say we're forewarned.

So we die in a crash
As if we were scorned.

So small was that sign
On the side of the road,

We may not get home
To our humble abode...

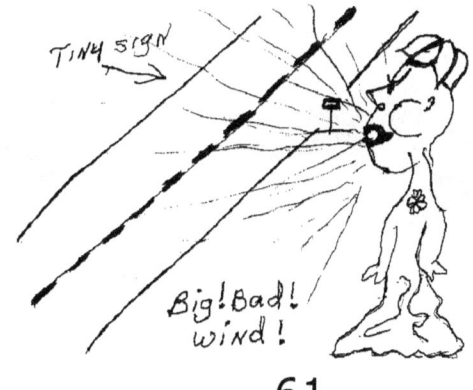

Patricia A Fisher

The Healing Of Nature

Hello ITSMEEE Again

THE HEALING OF NATURE

The current I feel
Pulls me away
Toward a place
I'd rather not be.

I'm afraid today!
    It made me this way.
The current
Won't let go of me!

I'm at the edge
    Of losing my self
For days and days
    At a time.

What's left for me
    Is writing, you see.
So here is my truth
    Put to rhyme.

Patricia A Fisher

I'm in a sort of prison
      That started before this place.
(In forest of green
      I am seldomly seen,
With a tear, or a frown,
      On my face.)

I look around at this beauty,
      And the sounds of people at play,
And the songs of birds.
      In so many words,
I'm writing my troubles away.

Hello ITSMEEE Again

God bless the wind and the weather,
    And the sunshine on these hills,
The smell of pine,
Like the taste of sweet wine,
    The cleansing of it fills

My heart with the essence of nature,
    And more beauty than words can say.
I no longer fear
    Those who are near,
My prison has faded away.

Patricia A Fisher

Now what's left is just freedom
    To live and love and be.
What was there before
    Is no more.
I've opened my eyes to see
    That hiding behind the fear
And woe
Lets little sunshine in.
    And being without happiness?
    Perhaps the greatest sin!

So hear me when I say to you
    Freedom can be found.
If we only look for it,
    Or listen for the sound.

It comes in the form of music
    Or sunshine on a hill
Or a lake of blue green water
    Serene and very still

Hello ITSMEEE Again

It's felt
    When a prayer is answered,
Or when we have a choice.

It's heard
    When we say
I love you –

Patricia A Fisher

The sound
     Of each soft voice.

So remove
     That prison
Around you.

Come out
     Wherever
You are!

The world
Will just
Astound you!

Your journey
Won't
Be far.

Hello ITSMEEE Again

Just look
Beyond
Your fear –

The rut
You may
Be in.

For being
Without
Happiness?

By far
The greatest
Sin!

Patricia A Fisher

HOME SICK PUP

A rat in a Bounder
They say it's a dog
With hair that sticks out
And a bark like a frog!

It makes so much noise
While it sits by the glass.
Its job seems to be
To yap and harass!

So worried and scared
Of its own little shadow.
It wants to go home
To Colorado!

Hello ITSMEEE Again

LITTLE BIRDIE

Little birdie, cheep, cheep, cheep,
Upon my windowsill.

The globs of gunk
And other junk

Are making you so ill.
When will we learn

We're ruining
Our water, air, and turf?

When will we learn
There's no "away?"
There's just our Mother Earth.

Patricia A Fisher

NATURE'S MUSIC

Sing to me sweet music,
Oh, forest with your trees
And tell me what your creatures
Have to say.

Did humans burn your branches?
And trample all your leaves?
And disrespect your ants and bugs
Today?

Oh, give me of your water
Of rain so softly fallen.
Give me sounds of birds
In song
I pray.

Hello ITSMEEE Again

For I will tell my story
Although not quite as sweet,
And drink of springs
That bubble from your clay.

I'm sitting here in wonder,
As the breezes play up high.
I try to say just how
This makes me feel.

There's no way I can tell you.
It's here for all to see.
It's something that you'll
Never have to steal.

What's that? Someone is calling
From a twig I see up there.
Someone so small, and now
In joyous song.

Patricia A Fisher

I guess I'll end this note to you,
A symphony now plays.
It beckons me.
And now I say, "So long."

Hello ITSMEEE Again

Patricia A Fisher

A GOLDEN MOMENT

Light was dancing
  On the underbranch,
Reflected
  From water below.

There were wealths
  Of diamonds
On the water's top
  God's putting on a show!

I sat for ages
  Or maybe an hour
Unheeded
  By sounds around,

Hello ITSMEEE Again

Except for my own
  Private
    Musical,
The songs
  And the
    Beauty
      I found.

My soul
  Was at rest,
During this time.
  It seemed like eternity.

God was there,
  A squirrel
    Or two.

And I,
  Myself
And me.

Patricia A Fisher

AGGRAVATION!

Dag-nabbed blackbirds!
No wonder
They baked 'em
In a pie!

They sound
Like a squeaky swing
Or a gate
That needs oil,
When they cry!

They squawk
And they squeak,
And they screech

In the trees
Beyond my reach,

Hello ITSMEEE Again

Or I'd take one down,
In the water I'd drown,
And then I'd make a speech.

"One less noisy blackbird,
Here in the water it floats.
One more peek
At the peace I seek.
I now can hear the notes,

Of robins with their red breast,
Of other lovely birds
I now can think.
My coffee I drink.
I listen without words.

To all the sounds of the forest,
With breezes blowing high.
To rustling leaves,
My heart only grieves
More blackbirds didn't die!

Patricia A Fisher

Here they come again!
Their groups of nine or ten!
The pitch so loud
That noisy crowd,
Same thing over again!

I guess I'll get a slingshot,
And practice with my aim,
So there will be less blackbirds.
Now won't **that** be a shame?

Hello ITSMEEE Again

You can't always get what you want,

You may just get what you need, and you *might even like it better…*

Patricia A Fisher

RACHEL AT 17

Dear Rachel, can you hear me?
You are so rare and good.

I wouldn't change
A thing about you,
Even if I could.

The pain you feel?
I've felt it!
Your rage and
Anger too.

It's all a part –
Cross my heart –
Of you just being you.

Hello ITSMEEE Again

One day you may stop wandering
From here
To way out there.

You may just find
You're not so blind.
You'll see
That we all care.

So be at rest my darling,
And ride the river through.

You need to know
We all are waiting
Just to be with you.

Patricia A Fisher

I've wondered from time to time just who this person is. I always come back to knowing that he is love.

He is 52 years older now, and he just never lost his innocence....

Hello ITSMEEE Again

THE "C" WORD

In my imagination
I sit in wonder of
Nothing and just everything –
What's this thing called love?

Mean words were said
Between us,
"You don't understand,
If you did, you'd say you're wrong!
Your head is in the sand!"

Now the minutes pass so slow.
My watch says 5 o'clock.
At noon we started arguing.
Why can't we just talk?

Patricia A Fisher

Marriage means not always
Believing every word.
It means a disagreement
Instead of what I've heard.

I've heard the elders on TV:
"A fight? We've had not one!
In 50 years of marriage
It's all been just great fun!"

Hello ITSMEEE Again

"We agree 'bout everything!"
I don't think it's true...
Someone must be missing!
There must not have been two!

If two of you agree so much,
Which one takes the rap?
Which one lets the other win?
Which one is the sap?

Which one has no words to say –
Nothing to believe in?
Just to let the other bray
Never saying, "I win!"

Well, I'm so smart here talking –
Intelligence immense!
So why do I
Just want to cry?
To fight does not make sense.

Patricia A Fisher

I don't know the answer –
What's this thing called love –
I guess it's when
We choose to care
In front of God above.

It's when we hear each other,
Although we disagree.
It's often this word *compromise*.
He gets his way then me …

Hello ITSMEEE Again

YOU CAN'T RUN FOREVER

You can't run forever,
So stay right here with me.
I'll tell you tales
About those days gone by,

About how much
I've loved you,
And wanted
You so near,

About the way
You never
Made me cry,

Patricia A Fisher

About how you
Would hold me.
You'd whisper
In my ear,

And tell me
Everything
To make me smile.

You'd keep the world
From entering
Our private
Rendezvous.

We'd dream and talk
And "be"
Just for a while.

Hello ITSMEEE Again

I've always been
Amazed by you,
Your truth so overflowing.

My faith in what
You'd say
Was so complete.

You've never been
Judgmental.
You equaled every man—
Never any trace of real conceit.

Patricia A Fisher

You now must know
I love you.
You now must
Stay in sight.

You now
Must run
No more
My dear
I cry.

For we have
Been together
Through times
That weren't so good.

We've earned the right
To never say goodbye.

Hello ITSMEEE Again

So be with me
My darling,
Though the sun
Is setting,

And silver gray
Is showing
In our hair.

We've come too far
To stop now –
To cut the ties
That bind.

We have a lot
More moments
We can share.

Patricia A Fisher

So, though our years
Turn golden,
Our bones begin
To creak,

Our bodies
Are not like
They used to be.

I'm glad I met you, darling –
The years have not been bad.
So, come, my love,
And sit right here with me.

Hello ITSMEEE Again

ONLY YESTERDAY

How did we grow old,
My man?

Let's see,
How could this be?

Like that yonder tree,
My man,

Standing
Tall and free,

It seems
That only yesterday,

Patricia A Fisher

When first
I spoke your name,

You spoke my name
Back to me.

My love,
We felt the same.

Twenty-seven years ago,
And more I think it be,

That we fell in love,
Old man,

I with you,
And you with me.

Hello ITSMEEE Again

That first day
You walked me home.

What did I think of this?

That first day
You gave to me

A handshake
Not a kiss!

I teased you so profusely.
We laughed. Yes, it is true.

This was the first of many
Times I laughed with you.

Patricia A Fisher

And then came pain –
A lot I think,
As life so often brings.

But through it all
We've shared so much
So many wondrous things.

We've had our friends
To see us through
When we just couldn't see,

The way for us
To move beyond
A rough and stormy sea.

Hello ITSMEEE Again

We've had the funds
To keep us fed
And clothe us in the weather.

We've so far had
Good fortune
That keeps us both together.

We've had our home
To shelter us
And bring the fam' to dine.

We've shared those
Christmas holidays
That kept us feeling fine.

Patricia A Fisher

But when I woke
Today, Old Man,
I saw you 'crost the room.

I knew that many
Years had past.
How did they go so soon?

Hello ITSMEEE Again

GOODBYE, MOM...

I then cried out, "Mom! Mom! Mom! I can't feel you any more! But I also can't think of your body deteriorating underground!"

Where the dead go is a mystery to me, and I am saddened by that.

Then, it was as if I came tearing through the ozone layer! I orbited Earth once, and came in for a landing among the Earthlings (as if I were an alien).

Now, I am an Earthling—limited and equal—yet different from other Earthlings.

Patricia A Fisher

Pain is different here. Never has it been so difficult expressing, and feeling, pain.

My heart is breaking, and all I can do is cry.

Then I feel warm inside the loving arms of my husband. I hear him whisper, "It'll be okay, it'll be okay."

As I say goodbye, again …

Hello ITSMEEE Again

EARTH: A PLACE BETWEEN HEAVEN AND HELL

Earth is such
A troubled place.
I wipe the tears
Off of my face,
    And start all over
again...

Since coming here,
I can't explain,
The happiness,
And awful pain,
The curse of
Feeling bad again,
    And I pick myself up...

Patricia A Fisher

They promise you
That all is well.
They'll be there
At the time they tell,
And on this Earth
It's buy and sell,
    And they don't call at
    all...

You're feeling fine
Today you say.
You have some plans
To go away.
But you can't go.
You have to stay,
    And you get
    disappointed...

Hello ITSMEEE Again

At noon that day
You try some more,
To move yourself
Right out the door.
But exercising
Is a bore.
    They say fresh air will do it...

For one whole hour
You feel fine.
You ask a friend
To come and dine.
But he's too busy
All the time.
    So you drop it...

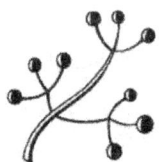

Patricia A Fisher

It's half past eight.
You've waited long.
You're humming
Your old favorite song.
Your appetite
Is going strong.
      You head for sugar...

It's television
Till you're tired.
You don't know
Just what transpired.
Go to bed,
Or you'll get fired!
      But you stay up
      anyway...

Hello ITSMEEE Again

You wake up
All in a heap.
You've made
A promise
You must keep.
But all you want
To do is sleep.
    Your job is waiting...

Patricia A Fisher

There is a constant
In you life,
To ease away
The pain and strife,

Far beyond
Our understanding.
Stronger than
A reprimanding.

Hello ITSMEEE Again

More than any
Thing I find,
To calm and soothe
A troubled mind.

It's love abundant
I am told.
More precious
Than a pot of gold.

Patricia A Fisher

Life on Earth
I have surmised
Is often ugly
And despised!

Except for when
We choose to care -
Making Earth
A place to share...

Hello ITSMEEE Again

They say that humor
Helps some too.
So you tell me,
And I tell you -
    A joke...

Truth comes in
Especially!
Lies spread far
Past you and me.
Tell it like
It had to be
    It clears your mind...

Patricia A Fisher

Love and humor,
Plus what's true,
Brings a peace
'Tween me and you.
Sprinkle in
Some bits of hope.
These are ways
To help us cope.
     And they bring joy...

Hello ITSMEEE Again

Add to this
A bit of rest,
For you to look
And feel your best.
You'll face the world
With extra zest!
    Now get going...

Patricia A Fisher

ABOUT THE AUTHOR

Photo of author at age 18 with a real bear!

Hello ITSMEEE Again

Patricia Fisher was born in Denver, Colorado where she lives with her husband, Dennis. She is fond of camping and hiking in her beloved RockyMountains, and she loves to write when inspired to do so.

Pat has suffered from a mental illness for 35 years, and she never stops hoping for peace of mind...
'Journaling in Rhyme' is a major tool for her! She has been using it since age 15.

Patricia A Fisher

Hello ITSMEEE Again

Patricia A Fisher

www.ingramcontent.com/pod-product-compliance
Lightning Source LLC
Chambersburg PA
CBHW071128090426
42736CB00012B/2052